To:

_____

From:

_____

Date:

_____

Visit Christian Art Gifts Inc. at www.christianartgifts.com

My Refuge and Strength

Published by Christian Art Gifts, Inc.

Previously published as
TouchPoints for Troubled Times: God's Answers for Your Daily Needs
First printing by Tyndale House Publishers in 2003.

General editors: Ronald A. Beers and V. Gilbert Beers
Managing editor: Linda Taylor
Contributing writers: V. Gilbert Beers, Ronald A. Beers, Brian R. Coffey, Jonathan D. Gray,
Shawn A. Harrison, Sanford D. Hull, Rhonda K. O'Brien, Douglas J. Rumford, Linda Taylor

Designed by Christian Art Gifts
Cover and interior images used under license from Shutterstock.com

Printed in China

ISBN 978-1-4321-3259-0

20 21 22 23 24 25 26 27 28 29 – 10 9 8 7 6 5 4 3 2 1

MY REFUGE

AND

STRENGTH

God's answers of comfort and assurance
for life's most challenging times

God is
our REFUGE
& STRENGTH,
always ready to help
in times of trouble.

Psalm 46:1

PREFACE

As we consider the tension in our world, we often cannot help but feel a tinge of fear. We look to the heavens and ask, "God, what are you up to?" We may even momentarily wonder if the God we look to as sovereign Creator hasn't, for a time, lost control.

It is just at those times that we must listen to his answer—the answer he gives us in the pages of his Word. What he is "up to" is no different from what he has been "up to" since time began. He continues to write the story of salvation in the lives of people all over the globe. Trouble and tension have existed in the world since time began—these days are really not that different—and the answers have always been in God's Word. There we find a God who is at once loving and merciful, yet also awesome in power and promising to right all wrongs forever.

In this book you will find questions on various topics that may touch your heart during these troubled times. Each topic is listed alphabetically—with questions, and Scripture passages. You can read through this book page by page or use it as a reference guide for topics of particular interest to you.

Our prayer is that you will continue to search God's Word deliberately and diligently. May you find God's answers, for he longs to be your daily guide. Enjoy your treasure hunt!

The Editors

All Scripture is inspired by God and is useful to teach us what is true and to make us realize what is wrong in our lives. It straightens us out and teaches us to do what is right. It is God's way of preparing us in every way, fully equipped for every good thing God wants us to do. 2 Timothy 3:16-17

ABSENCE

Be sure of this: I am with you always,
even to the end of the age. Matthew 28:20

WHY DO I SOMETIMES FEEL THAT GOD IS ABSENT?
I NEED TO FEEL HIM CLOSE TODAY, BUT I DON'T FEEL
HIM AT ALL.

O LORD , why do you stand so far away? Why do you hide
when I need you the most? PSALM 10:1

The greater your troubles, the farther away God sometimes seems.
In your darkest hour, you may feel that God is hiding. You must
have faith in his promise to always be with you. Don't trust your
feelings; trust God and his promises to you.

You know when I sit down or stand up. You know my every
thought … I can never escape from your spirit! I can never
get away from your presence! PSALM 139:2, 7

Even when I walk through the dark valley of death, I will not
be afraid, for you are close beside me. PSALM 23:4

God never promised that by believing in him your life would be
free from trouble. He does not promise to take you around the
dark valley, but he does promise to walk with you through it.

ADVERSITY

*When you go through deep waters and great trouble, I will
be with you ... For I am the Lord, your God. Isaiah 43:2-3*

IS GOD LISTENING WHEN I CRY OUT BECAUSE OF MY TROUBLES? DOES HE REALLY HEAR, AND DOES HE CARE?

I cried out to the Lord in my great trouble, and he answered
me. I called to you from the world of the dead, and Lord,
you heard me! JONAH 2:2

WILL BEING FAITHFUL TO GOD SPARE ME FROM ADVERSITY?

Pharaoh sent this order to the slave drivers ... "Do not
supply the [Israelites] with any more straw for making
bricks. Let them get it themselves! ... They obviously don't
have enough to do. If they did, they wouldn't be talking
about going into the wilderness to offer sacrifices to their
God." EXODUS 5:6-8

*When you believe in Jesus, Satan becomes your enemy. He will
try to stop you from following God by giving you all manner of
adversity. He hopes that he can at least make you doubt God and
be unable to witness for him. Continue to be faithful, even through
times of adversity.*

ASSURANCE

But blessed are those who trust in the LORD and have made the LORD their hope and confidence. They are like trees planted along a riverbank, with roots that reach deep into the water. Such trees are not bothered by the heat or worried by long months of drought. Their leaves stay green, and they go right on producing delicious fruit. Jeremiah 17:7-8

WHERE CAN I FIND ASSURANCE AMID THE UNCERTAINTIES OF LIFE? CAN I BE SURE OF ANYTHING?

Through Christ you have come to trust in God. And because God raised Christ from the dead and gave him great glory, your faith and hope can be placed confidently in God. 1 PETER 1:21

Can anything ever separate us from Christ's love? Does it mean he no longer loves us if we have trouble or calamity? … I am convinced that nothing can ever separate us from his love … Our fears for today, our worries about tomorrow, and even the powers of hell can't keep God's love away. ROMANS 8:35, 38-39

God is the only one in whom you can completely trust without fear of disappointment. You can be assured that what he says is true and what he does is reliable. The world is filled with uncertainty, but you can trust in God's sure promises.

BLESSINGS

How we praise God, the Father of our Lord Jesus Christ, who has blessed us with every spiritual blessing in the heavenly realms because we belong to Christ. Ephesians 1:3

IF GOD PROMISES TO BLESS HIS PEOPLE, WHY IS LIFE SOMETIMES SO FULL OF TROUBLE?

The apostles left the high council rejoicing that God had counted them worthy to suffer dishonor for the name of Jesus. ACTS 5:41

God blesses the people who patiently endure testing. JAMES 1:12

Sometimes great blessings come out of great trouble because these trials deepen your relationship with the Lord, which is the greatest blessing of all.

HOW CAN THE PROMISE OF BLESSING HELP ME WHEN I AM WEARY OR DISCOURAGED?

Don't get tired of doing what is good. Don't get discouraged and give up, for we will reap a harvest of blessing at the appropriate time. GALATIANS 6:9

When you are tempted to give up, new resolve comes from remembering that God promises to bring a harvest of blessing in his perfect time.

BROKENHEARTED

*He lifted me out of the pit of despair, out of the mud
and the mire. He set my feet on solid ground and
steadied me as I walked along. Psalm 40:2*

HOW DOES GOD RESPOND TO THE BROKENHEARTED?

The LORD is close to the brokenhearted; he rescues those
who are crushed in spirit. PSALM 34:18

He heals the brokenhearted, binding up their wounds.
PSALM 147:3

I AM BROKENHEARTED. WHAT SHOULD I DO?

Come quickly, LORD, and answer me, for my depression
deepens. Don't turn away from me, or I will die. Let me
hear of your unfailing love to me in the morning, for I am
trusting you. Show me where to walk, for I have come to
you in prayer. PSALM 143:7-8

He comforts us in all our troubles so that we can comfort
others. When others are troubled, we will be able to give
them the same comfort God has given us.
2 CORINTHIANS 1:4

*Look to the Word of God for help. Meditate on God's character,
promises, and commitment to you. He who created the universe
by his word can re-create a new spirit within you. His Word will
comfort and encourage you.*

CARING

*Give all your worries and cares to God, for he cares
about what happens to you.* 1 Peter 5:7

DOES GOD CARE WHAT HAPPENS TO ME?

You have been with me from birth; from my mother's womb
you have cared for me. No wonder I am always praising you!
PSALM 71:6

I am overcome with joy because of your unfailing love, for
you have seen my troubles, and you care about the anguish
of my soul. PSALM 31:7

HOW DOES GOD SHOW HIS CARE FOR ME?

The LORD keeps you from all evil and preserves your life.
The LORD keeps watch over you as you come and go, both
now and forever. PSALM 121:7-8

The LORD is close to all who call on him, yes, to all who
call on him sincerely. He fulfills the desires of those who
fear him; he hears their cries for help and rescues them. The
LORD protects all those who love him, but he destroys the
wicked. PSALM 145:18-20

And if God cares so wonderfully for flowers that are here
today and gone tomorrow, won't he more surely care for
you? You have so little faith! MATTHEW 6:30

He comforts us
in all our troubles
so that we
can comfort
OTHERS.
When others are troubled,
we will be able
to give them the
SAME COMFORT
God has given us.

2 Corinthians 1:4

CHALLENGES

Be strong and very courageous. Obey all the laws Moses gave you. Do not turn away from them, and you will be successful in everything you do ... I command you—be strong and courageous! Do not be afraid or discouraged. For the LORD your God is with you wherever you go. Joshua 1:7, 9

IN A WORLD THAT SEEMS OPPOSED TO GOD, HOW DO I HANDLE THE CHALLENGE OF KEEPING MY FAITH STRONG?

God has given us both his promise and his oath. These two things are unchangeable because it is impossible for God to lie. Therefore, we who have fled to him for refuge can take new courage, for we can hold on to his promise with confidence. HEBREWS 6:18

The strength to handle challenges comes from God alone. Therefore you must stay close to him through Bible study and prayer, never doubting his promises.

HOW CAN I POSSIBLY FACE TODAY'S CHALLENGES?

In your strength I can crush an army; with my God I can scale any wall. 2 SAMUEL 22:30

Now glory be to God! By his mighty power at work within us, he is able to accomplish infinitely more than we would ever dare to ask or hope. EPHESIANS 3:20

CHANGE

God is not a man, that he should lie. He is not a human, that he should change his mind. Has he ever spoken and failed to act? Has he ever promised and not carried it through? Numbers 23:19

WITH ALL THE CHANGE IN MY LIFE, HOW CAN I KEEP IT ALL TOGETHER?

You [God] are always the same. HEBREWS 1:12

Jesus Christ is the same yesterday, today, and forever. HEBREWS 13:8

You can trust the character of God to be unchanging and reliable. No matter how much your life changes, no matter what new situations you face, God goes with you—and he never changes.

Heaven and earth will disappear, but my words will remain forever. MARK 13:31

And we know that God causes everything to work together for the good of those who love God and are called according to his purpose for them. ROMANS 8:28

Sometimes change seems to be for the worse. At those times, you may feel as if you're going to fall apart. When such change occurs, remember that God can work his will even through traumatic, unpredictable, and unfair change. Nothing takes him by surprise. No change occurs that he cannot redeem.

CHAOS

For the LORD is God, and he created the heavens and earth and put everything in place. He made the world to be lived in, not to be a place of empty chaos. "I am the LORD," he says, "and there is no other." Isaiah 45:18

THE WORLD SEEMS TO BE IN COMPLETE CHAOS. HOW CAN I FIND ORDER AND PEACE IN MY INNER SPIRIT?

May God bless you with his special favor and wonderful peace as you come to know Jesus, our God and Lord, better and better. 2 PETER 1:2

Since we have been made right in God's sight by faith, we have peace with God because of what Jesus Christ our Lord has done for us. ROMANS 5:1

You have been given peace as a result of your relationship with Jesus. So partake of that gift.

And now I make one more appeal, my dear brothers and sisters. Watch out for people who cause divisions and upset people's faith by teaching things that are contrary to what you have been taught. Stay away from them. ROMANS 16:17

Guard what you hear and believe; watch the company that you keep. Chaos is often the result of not being diligent in avoiding that which causes strife and division in your life.

CIRCUMSTANCES

When darkness overtakes the godly, light will come bursting in. They are generous, compassionate, and righteous ... Such people will not be overcome by evil circumstances. Those who are righteous will be long remembered. They do not fear bad news; they confidently trust the LORD to care for them. They are confident and fearless and can face their foes triumphantly. Psalm 112:4, 6-8

HOW SHOULD I RESPOND TO LIFE'S SOMETIMES TROUBLING CIRCUMSTANCES?

Don't worry about anything; instead, pray about everything. Tell God what you need, and thank him for all he has done. PHILIPPIANS 4:6

HOW CAN I MAKE THE MOST OF MY CIRCUMSTANCES?

Blessed are those who trust in the LORD and have made the LORD their hope and confidence. They are like trees planted along a riverbank, with roots that reach deep into the water. Such trees are not bothered by the heat or worried by long months of drought. Their leaves stay green, and they go right on producing delicious fruit. JEREMIAH 17:7-8

Trust in the Lord; he is worthy of your hope and confidence. Those who trust in the Lord understand the secret of his life-sustaining power.

Don't worry
about anything;
instead,
PRAY
about
everything.

Tell
GOD
what you need,
& thank
# HIM
for all he has done.

Philippians 4:6

COMFORT

May our Lord Jesus Christ ... who ... gave us everlasting comfort and good hope, comfort your hearts and give you strength in every good thing you do and say. 2 Thessalonians 2:16-17

IN MY TIMES OF DISTRESS, WILL GOD COMFORT ME?

But whenever you were in distress and turned to the LORD, the God of Israel, and sought him out, you found him. 2 CHRONICLES 15:4

Your need for comfort and God's supply of comfort are always in perfect balance.

He will feed his flock like a shepherd. He will carry the lambs in his arms ... [and] gently lead the mother sheep with their young. ISAIAH 40:11

IN WHAT WAYS WILL I RECEIVE COMFORT FROM GOD?

God blesses those who mourn, for they will be comforted. MATTHEW 5:4

Don't be afraid, for I am with you. Do not be dismayed, for I am your God. I will strengthen you. I will help you. I will uphold you with my victorious right hand. ISAIAH 41:10

Do not be afraid, for I am with you and will bless you. GENESIS 26:24

CONFUSION

God is not a God of disorder but of peace. 1 Corinthians 14:33

THE WORLD IS A PRETTY CONFUSING PLACE RIGHT NOW. HOW SHOULD I DEAL WITH LIFE'S CONFUSION?

When doubts filled my mind, your comfort gave me renewed hope and cheer. PSALM 94:19

We are pressed on every side by troubles, but we are not crushed and broken. We are perplexed, but we don't give up and quit. 2 CORINTHIANS 4:8

HOW SHOULD I RESPOND WHEN GOD CONFUSES ME— WHEN I DON'T UNDERSTAND HIM?

Without wavering, let us hold tightly to the hope we say we have, for God can be trusted to keep his promise. HEBREWS 10:23

This salvation was something the prophets wanted to know more about. They prophesied about this gracious salvation prepared for you, even though they had many questions as to what it all could mean. 1 PETER 1:10

Respond in obedience regardless of your level of understanding. You need not know everything about plumbing to take a bath. You need not know everything about God to follow him.

CONVICTIONS

Be on guard. Stand true to what you believe.
Be courageous. Be strong. 1 Corinthians 16:13

HOW CAN I DEVELOP GODLY CONVICTIONS?

He guards the paths of justice and protects those who are faithful to him. Then you will understand what is right, just, and fair, and you will know how to find the right course of action every time. PROVERBS 2:8-9

Listen to me, you who know right from wrong and cherish my law in your hearts. Do not be afraid of people's scorn or their slanderous talk. ISAIAH 51:7

The godly offer good counsel; they know what is right from wrong. PSALM 37:30

WHY IS IT IMPORTANT TO HAVE CONVICTIONS? HOW DO GODLY CONVICTIONS HELP ME?

But Daniel made up his mind not to defile himself by eating the food and wine given to them by the king. He asked the chief official for permission to eat other things instead. DANIEL 1:8

Living by your convictions helps you resist temptation.

But I lavish my love on those who love me and obey my commands, even for a thousand generations. EXODUS 20:6

Having godly convictions helps you experience God's love.

COPING

He gives power to those who are tired and worn out;
he offers strength to the weak. Isaiah 40:29

HOW DO I COPE WHEN LIFE'S PAIN BECOMES OVERWHELMING?

The LORD helps the fallen and lifts up those bent beneath their loads. PSALM 145:14

When you go through deep waters and great trouble, I will be with you. When you go through rivers of difficulty, you will not drown! When you walk through the fire of oppression, you will not be burned up; the flames will not consume you. ISAIAH 43:2

Give your burdens to the LORD, and he will take care of you. He will not permit the godly to slip and fall. PSALM 55:22

HOW DO I COPE WHEN LIFE'S DEMANDS SEEM IMPOSSIBLE?

For I can do everything with the help of Christ who gives me the strength I need. PHILIPPIANS 4:13

He comforts us in all our troubles so that we can comfort others. When others are troubled, we will be able to give them the same comfort God has given us. 2 CORINTHIANS 1:4

COURAGE

You will have courage because you will have hope. Job 11:18

WHERE DO I GET THE COURAGE TO GO ON WHEN LIFE SEEMS TOO HARD OR OBSTACLES SEEM TOO BIG?

The LORD is my light and my salvation—so why should I be afraid? PSALM 27:1

Don't be afraid, for I am with you. Do not be dismayed, for I am your God. I will strengthen you. I will help you. I will uphold you with my victorious right hand. ISAIAH 41:10

HOW DO I FIND THE COURAGE TO FACE CHANGE?

Do not be afraid to go down to Egypt, for I will see to it that you become a great nation there. GENESIS 46:3

Change may be part of God's plan for you. If so, what you are headed into will give you joy and satisfaction beyond your expectations. Remember, the greatest advances in life come through change.

When Ishbosheth heard about Abner's death at Hebron, he lost all courage, and his people were paralyzed with fear. 2 SAMUEL 4:1

If you take all of your courage from another person, you will eventually be left with nothing when that person is gone. If you trust in God, you will have the strength to go on.

CRISIS

God is our refuge and strength, always ready
to help in times of trouble. Psalm 46:1

WHERE IS GOD IN MY TIME OF CRISIS?

He lifted me out of the pit of despair, out of the mud and the mire. He set my feet on solid ground and steadied me as I walked along. PSALM 40:2

I [Jesus] have told you all this so that you may have peace in me. Here on earth you will have many trials and sorrows. But take heart, because I have overcome the world. JOHN 16:33

God does not say he will always prevent crisis in our lives—we all live in a sinful world where terrible things happen—but God does promise to always be there with you, helping you through any crisis. Trust in his promises.

HOW SHOULD I RESPOND TO MY CRISIS?

When I had lost all hope, I turned my thoughts once more to the LORD. JONAH 2:7

Have mercy on me, O God, have mercy! I look to you for protection. I will hide beneath the shadow of your wings until this violent storm is past. PSALM 57:1

In a time of crisis you may wonder, Who can I trust? You can always trust the Lord.

Don't be afraid,
for I am with you.
Don't be discouraged, for
I AM YOUR GOD.
I will strengthen you
and *help* you.
I will hold you up with my
victorious right hand.

Isaiah 41:10

DEATH

*But as for me, God will redeem my life. He will snatch
me from the power of death. Psalm 49:15*

HOW DO I KEEP A PROPER PERSPECTIVE ABOUT DEATH?
WHY AM I SO AFRAID OF IT?

For to me, living is for Christ, and dying is even better.
PHILIPPIANS 1:21

*A fear of death may be an indication of a weak relationship with
God. You must be ready to die—looking forward to being in the
presence of the Lord.*

Since you have been raised to new life with Christ, set your
sights on the realities of heaven ... Let heaven fill your
thoughts. COLOSSIANS 3:1-2

HOW CAN I BE CERTAIN THAT THERE IS ETERNAL LIFE?

But the fact is that Christ has been raised from the dead. He
has become the first of a great harvest of those who will be
raised to life again. 1 CORINTHIANS 15:20

*Resurrection life is not just a theory. Jesus' resurrection guarantees
the resurrection of everyone who trusts in him.*

For God so loved the world that he gave his only Son, so
that everyone who believes in him will not perish, but have
eternal life. JOHN 3:16

DEPRESSION

Then Jesus said, "Come to me, all of you who are weary and carry heavy burdens, and I will give you rest." Matthew 11:28

I FEEL DEPRESSED AND IT SEEMS LIKE GOD DOESN'T CARE. DOES HE CARE ABOUT HOW LOW I FEEL?

Even in darkness I cannot hide from you. PSALM 139:12

From the depths of despair, O LORD, I call for your help. PSALM 130:1

You can cry out to God in prayer even during the darkest night of despair. He will hear you.

He was despised and rejected—a man of sorrows, acquainted with bitterest grief. ISAIAH 53:3

Remember that Christ understands the pain of human life.

Nothing in all creation will ever be able to separate us from the love of God that is revealed in Christ Jesus our Lord. ROMANS 8:39

HOW SHOULD I HANDLE DEPRESSION?

Come quickly, LORD, and answer me, for my depression deepens. Don't turn away from me, or I will die. PSALM 143:7

LORD, you know the hopes of the helpless. Surely you will listen to their cries and comfort them. PSALM 10:17

DESPAIR

Give all your worries and cares to God, for he cares about what happens to you. 1 Peter 5:7

I SOMETIMES THINK I'M LOSING IT. THE PAIN IS SO INTENSE, THE HURT SO DEEP. HOW CAN GOD HELP ME IN THIS TIME OF DESPAIR?

But in my distress I cried out to the LORD; yes, I called to my God for help. He heard me from his sanctuary; my cry reached his ears. 2 SAMUEL 22:7

God listens and cares about you, so never stop talking to him through prayer.

Why am I discouraged? Why so sad? I will put my hope in God! I will praise him again—my Savior and my God! PSALM 42:5

When Jesus heard about it he said, "Lazarus's sickness will not end in death. No, it is for the glory of God. I, the Son of God, will receive glory from this." JOHN 11:4

God sends his help no matter how hopeless the circumstances seem. He is the God of the impossible.

"I know the plans I have for you," says the LORD. "They are plans for good and not for disaster, to give you a future and a hope." JEREMIAH 29:11

God gives a hope-filled future. Depend on him!

DISAPPOINTMENT

Give your burdens to the LORD, and he
will take care of you. Psalm 55:22

HOW SHOULD I HANDLE MY DISAPPOINTMENT WITH GOD?

Three different times I begged the Lord to take it away. Each time he said, "My gracious favor is all you need. My power works best in your weakness." So now I am glad to boast about my weaknesses, so that the power of Christ may work through me ... For when I am weak, then I am strong. 2 CORINTHIANS 12:8-10

Remember that although you may not understand why God doesn't always take away your pain, your weaknesses are great opportunities for God to work his power through you.

HOW SHOULD I DEAL WITH LIFE'S DISAPPOINTMENTS?

O God, you are my God; I earnestly search for you. My soul thirsts for you. PSALM 63:1

In your disappointment, move toward God, not away from him. Running from the one who can help you is not wise.

And we know that God causes everything to work together for the good of those who love God and are called according to his purpose for them. ROMANS 8:28

Accept God's ability to still bring good.

DISCOURAGEMENT

He will remove all of their sorrows, and there will be no more death or sorrow or crying or pain. Revelation 21:4

HOW CAN I HANDLE DISCOURAGEMENT?

Hannah was in deep anguish, crying bitterly as she prayed to the LORD. 1 SAMUEL 1:10

Prayer is the first step you must take when discouraged, for it moves you into the presence of God.

Don't be discouraged by this mighty army, for the battle is not yours, but God's. 2 CHRONICLES 20:15

It would have been easy for the people of Judah to see only the vast enemy army and not see God standing by to destroy it. Discouragement can cause you to doubt God's love, drawing you away from the source of your greatest help.

HOW DOES GOD HELP ME WHEN I AM DISCOURAGED?

I command you—be strong and courageous! Do not be afraid or discouraged. For the LORD your God is with you wherever you go. JOSHUA 1:9

When the world hates you, remember it hated me before it hated you. JOHN 15:18

I lie in the dust, completely discouraged; revive me by your word ... I weep with grief; encourage me by your word. PSALM 119:25, 28

DOUBT

For God has said, "I will never fail you.
I will never forsake you." Hebrews 13:5

WHAT SHOULD I DO WHEN I FIND MYSELF DOUBTING?

The father instantly replied, "I do believe, but help me not to doubt!" MARK 9:24

Pray that God will give you the fullness of faith that you need.

Why are you so worried about having no food? ... Don't you remember anything at all? What about the five thousand men I fed with five loaves of bread? MARK 8:17-19

When you are struggling with experiential doubt, take time to remember the way God has worked in the Bible and in your life. Then you will grow confident that he is real and will work in your present situation.

Encourage each other and build each other up, just as you are already doing. 1 THESSALONIANS 5:11

Let us not neglect our meeting together. HEBREWS 10:25

When you are wrestling with doubt, keep attending church and stay close to other Christians. Resist the temptation to isolate yourself, for that will only serve to weaken your faith more. Doubt feeds on loneliness.

I command you –

be strong

and

COURAGEOUS!

Do not be afraid
or discouraged.

FOR THE LORD

your *God*

is with you
wherever you go.

Joshua 1:9

EMOTIONS

But when the Holy Spirit controls our lives, he will produce this kind of fruit in us: love, joy, peace, patience, kindness, goodness, faithfulness, gentleness, and self-control. Galatians 5:22-23

DURING THESE TROUBLED TIMES, I FEEL SO EMOTIONAL. IS IT OKAY TO BE OPEN WITH MY EMOTIONS?

The king was overcome with emotion. He went up to his room over the gateway and burst into tears. And as he went, he cried, "O my son Absalom! My son, my son Absalom! If only I could have died instead of you! O Absalom, my son, my son." 2 SAMUEL 18:33

It is not a sign of weakness to display your emotions. It is, rather, a sign of your humanity and an important component of your emotional health.

I cannot keep from speaking. I must express my anguish. I must complain in my bitterness. JOB 7:11

Keep an open dialogue with the Lord and others you trust so you are not covering up your emotions.

He told them, "My soul is crushed with grief to the point of death. Stay here and watch with me." MATTHEW 26:38

Jesus was honest with his disciples about his deep emotions. You also need this openness with trusted friends.

EMPATHY

When others are happy, be happy with them.
If they are sad, share their sorrow. Romans 12:15

WHAT IS EMPATHY?

Then, besides all this, I have the daily burden of how the churches are getting along. Who is weak without my feeling that weakness? Who is led astray, and I do not burn with anger? 2 CORINTHIANS 11:28-29

Empathy is deeply identifying with another's pain or position and responding with a desire to bring comfort.

HOW CAN I BE MORE EMPATHETIC TOWARD OTHERS?

All praise to the God and Father of our Lord Jesus Christ. He is the source of every mercy and the God who comforts us. He comforts us in all our troubles so that we can comfort others. When others are troubled, we will be able to give them the same comfort God has given us. 2 CORINTHIANS 1:3-4

Do for others as you would like them to do for you. LUKE 6:31

You can minister in ways you would like to be ministered to in similar circumstances. When you don't know what to do, ask yourself what you would want someone to do for you in that situation.

ENCOURAGEMENT

May our Lord Jesus Christ and God our Father ...
comfort your hearts and give you strength in every
good thing you do and say. 2 Thessalonians 2:16-17

HOW DOES GOD ENCOURAGE ME?

When I pray, you answer me; you encourage me by giving me the strength I need. PSALM 138:3

I lie in the dust, completely discouraged; revive me by your word. I weep with grief; encourage me by your word. PSALM 119:25, 28

HOW CAN I BE AN ENCOURAGEMENT TO OTHERS?

Don't use foul or abusive language. Let everything you say be good and helpful, so that your words will be an encouragement to those who hear them. EPHESIANS 4:29

By making sure everything you say is kind and uplifting.

Hezekiah encouraged the Levites for the skill they displayed as they served the LORD. 2 CHRONICLES 30:22

By complimenting them for a job well done.

A cheerful look brings joy to the heart; good news makes for good health. PROVERBS 15:30

By smiling!

ENDURANCE

Dear brothers and sisters, whenever trouble comes your way, let it be an opportunity for joy. For when your faith is tested, your endurance has a chance to grow. So let it grow, for when your endurance is fully developed, you will be strong in character and ready for anything. James 1:2-4

IN WHAT AREAS SHOULD I DEVELOP ENDURANCE?

My steps have stayed on your path; I have not wavered from following you. PSALM 17:5

So don't get tired of doing what is good. Don't get discouraged and give up, for we will reap a harvest of blessing at the appropriate time. GALATIANS 6:9

In doing good. It is difficult to do good over a long period of time when life throws you so many trials and temptations. An enduring faith, however, is up to the challenge.

HOW DO I DEVELOP ENDURANCE?

May God, who gives this patience and encouragement, help you live in complete harmony with each other—each with the attitude of Christ Jesus toward the other. ROMANS 15:5

Use every piece of God's armor to resist the enemy in the time of evil, so that after the battle you will still be standing firm. EPHESIANS 6:13

When I pray,
you answer me; you
encourage me
by giving me the
strength I need.

Psalm 138:3

ENEMIES

When you go out to fight your enemies and you face horses and chariots and an army greater than your own, do not be afraid. The LORD your God, who brought you safely out of Egypt, is with you! Deuteronomy 20:1

AS CHRISTIANS, WE KNOW THERE ARE MANY PEOPLE WHO CONSIDER THEMSELVES OUR ENEMIES. HOW DO THOSE ENEMIES TRY TO HURT US?

Then the LORD said to Moses, "Attack the Midianites and destroy them, because they assaulted you with deceit by tricking you into worshiping Baal of Peor." NUMBERS 25:16-18

By trying to lead believers into sin.

The leaders of the Philistines went to her and said, "Find out from Samson what makes him so strong and how he can be overpowered and tied up securely. Then each of us will give you eleven hundred pieces of silver." JUDGES 16:5

By finding our vulnerability and trying to use it against us.

WHERE CAN I TURN WHEN I FEEL OVERWHELMED BY THOSE WHO ARE WORKING AGAINST ME—MY ENEMIES?

O LORD, you are my refuge; never let me be disgraced. Rescue me! Save me from my enemies, for you are just. PSALM 71:1-2

EVIL

Then the Devil, who betrayed them, was thrown into the lake of fire that burns with sulfur, joining the beast and the false prophet. There they will be tormented day and night forever and ever. Revelation 20:10

WHERE DOES EVIL COME FROM?

The human heart is most deceitful and desperately wicked. Who really knows how bad it is? JEREMIAH 17:9

Our own hearts, polluted by sin and selfishness, are the source of much that is evil.

For we are not fighting against people made of flesh and blood, but against the evil rulers and authorities of the unseen world, against those mighty powers of darkness who rule this world, and against wicked spirits in the heavenly realms. EPHESIANS 6:12

Cosmic forces of evil, led by Satan, are engaged in a deadly rebellion against God.

HOW CAN I COMBAT EVIL?

Hate what is wrong. Stand on the side of good. ROMANS 12:9

A final word: Be strong with the Lord's mighty power. Put on all of God's armor so that you will be able to stand firm against all strategies and tricks of the Devil. EPHESIANS 6:10-11

FAITH

You will be among those praising him on that day, for you believed what we testified about him. 2 Thessalonians 1:10

WHY SHOULD I HAVE FAITH IN GOD?

I assure you, those who listen to my message and believe in God who sent me have eternal life. JOHN 5:24

Faith is the only way to get to heaven. It is the only doorway to eternal life. If God created eternity, then only through God can you get there.

What is faith? It is the confident assurance that what we hope for is going to happen. HEBREWS 11:1

Faith gives us hope. When the world seems to be a crazy, mixed-up place, believers can rest in the fact that one day God will come and make it all right. Our faith in his promise to do that someday allows us to keep going today.

HOW CAN I STRENGTHEN MY FAITH?

I honor and love your commands. I meditate on your principles ... Your principles have been the music of my life throughout the years of my pilgrimage. PSALM 119:48, 54

Your faith will grow stronger as you study the Bible and reflect on the truths.

FAITHFULNESS

He is the Rock; his work is perfect. Everything he does is just and fair. He is a faithful God who does no wrong; how just and upright he is! Deuteronomy 32:4

IS GOD FAITHFUL?

All heaven will praise your miracles, LORD; myriads of angels will praise you for your faithfulness. PSALM 89:5

He is the faithful God who keeps his covenant for a thousand generations. DEUTERONOMY 7:9

But the Lord is faithful; he will make you strong and guard you from the evil one. 2 THESSALONIANS 3:3

God is completely faithful. His faithfulness is so great it makes the angels sing!

IN WHAT WAYS DOES GOD SHOW HIS FAITHFULNESS?

Praise the Lord, the God of Israel, because he has visited his people and redeemed them. He has sent us a mighty Savior from the royal line of his servant David, just as he promised through his holy prophets long ago. LUKE 1:68-70

The LORD will answer when I call to him. PSALM 4:3

Hear my prayer, O LORD; listen to my plea! Answer me because you are faithful and righteous. PSALM 143:1

When you call on God, he faithfully answers.

He is the

Rock;

his work is

PERFECT.

Everything he does
is just and fair.

He is a

FAITHFUL

God

who does no wrong;
how just and upright he is!

Deuteronomy 32:4

FAREWELLS

And be sure of this: I am with you always,
even to the end of the age. Matthew 28:20

WHAT WILL HELP ME SAY GOOD-BYE IN A HEALTHY AND POSITIVE WAY?

When he had finished speaking, he knelt and prayed with them. They wept aloud as they embraced him in farewell, sad most of all because he had said that they would never see him again. ACTS 20:36-38

Praying together and being open and honest about the pain of parting are important to healthy good-byes.

HOW SHOULD I BID OTHERS FAREWELL? WHAT CAN MAKE A FAREWELL EASIER?

At last Jonathan said to David, "Go in peace, for we have made a pact in the LORD's name. We have entrusted each other and each other's children into the LORD's hands forever." Then David left, and Jonathan returned to the city. 1 SAMUEL 20:42

Entrusting the other person into God's care while you are gone.

FEAR

Don't be afraid, for I am with you. Do not be dismayed, for I am your God. I will strengthen you. I will help you. I will uphold you with my victorious right hand. Isaiah 41:10

THESE ARE FRIGHTENING TIMES. WHAT CAN I DO WHEN I AM OVERCOME WITH FEAR?

How we praise God, the Father of our Lord Jesus Christ, who has blessed us with every spiritual blessing in the heavenly realms. EPHESIANS 1:3

The Lord God will shine on them. And they will reign forever and ever. REVELATION 22:5

Remind yourself that as a Christian, your destiny is victory! The troubles of this world are only temporary. You can go forward with the confidence that you are on the winning side.

Don't worry about anything; instead, pray about everything. Tell God what you need, and thank him for all he has done. If you do this, you will experience God's peace, which is far more wonderful than the human mind can understand. His peace will guard your hearts and minds as you live in Christ Jesus. PHILIPPIANS 4:6-7

Pray with a thankful heart, asking God to give you what you need to deal with your fears.

FORGIVENESS

*With my authority, take this message of repentance
to all the nations, beginning in Jerusalem: "There is
forgiveness of sins for all who turn to me."* Luke 24:47

**I THINK I NEED TO MAKE THINGS RIGHT WITH GOD,
BUT I DON'T UNDERSTAND HIS FORGIVENESS. WHAT
DOES IT REALLY MEAN TO BE FORGIVEN?**

Perhaps he will forgive your evil thoughts, for I can see that
you are ... held captive by sin. ACTS 8:22-23

Forgiveness frees you from slavery to sin.

Love your enemies! Pray for those who persecute you!
MATTHEW 5:44

*Forgiveness paves the way for harmonious relationships, even with
your enemies.*

**HOW CAN I FORGIVE SOMEONE WHO HAS HURT ME
VERY BADLY?**

Get rid of all bitterness, rage, anger, harsh words, and slander,
as well as all types of malicious behavior. EPHESIANS 4:31

*Remember that unforgiveness not only ruins your relationships, it
also poisons your soul.*

Instead, be kind to one another, forgiving each other, just as
God through Christ has forgiven you. EPHESIANS 4:32

FUTURE

That is what the Scriptures mean when they say, "No eye has seen, no ear has heard, and no mind has imagined what God has prepared for those who love him." 1 Corinthians 2:9

HOW CAN I FACE THE FUTURE WHEN IT IS SO UNCERTAIN?

The LORD keeps watch over you as you come and go, both now and forever. PSALM 121:8

You can face the uncertain future because you have an unchanging God who loves and guides you. As the old saying puts it: We know not what the future holds, but we know who holds the future.

Here on earth you will have many trials and sorrows. But take heart, because I have overcome the world. JOHN 16:33

Jesus never promised a problem-free life; in fact, he promised just the opposite. So don't be surprised or fearful in hard times. Jesus is greater than any problem you will ever encounter.

So don't worry about tomorrow, for tomorrow will bring its own worries. Today's trouble is enough for today. MATTHEW 6:34

Most of the things we worry might happen never do. So don't waste time on the "what if" worries. Spend your worry time as prayer time.

GRIEF

The LORD is close to the brokenhearted; he rescues those who are crushed in spirit. Psalm 34:18

SOMETHING TERRIBLE HAS HAPPENED, LORD. I NEED YOU TO MINISTER TO ME. HOW WILL YOU DO THAT?

But you do see the trouble and grief they cause. You take note of it and punish them. The helpless put their trust in you. You are the defender of orphans. PSALM 10:14

God ministers to you through his personal attention.

Even when I walk through the dark valley of death, I will not be afraid, for you are close beside me. Your rod and your staff protect and comfort me. PSALM 23:4

God ministers to you through his comforting presence.

HOW DO I GET OVER MY GRIEF?

There is a time for everything, a season for every activity under heaven ... A time to cry and a time to laugh. A time to grieve and a time to dance. ECCLESIASTES 3:1, 4

Grief has its season, and its season may last a long while. But eventually God will lead you to move on and comfort others.

He will remove all of their sorrows, and there will be no more death or sorrow or crying or pain. REVELATION 21:4

Take hope that there will be no more grief in heaven.

HAND OF GOD

O Lord my God, you have done many miracles for us. Your plans for us are too numerous to list. If I tried to recite all your wonderful deeds, I would never come to the end of them. Psalm 40:5

I DON'T SEE MUCH EVIDENCE OF "THE HAND OF GOD" IN THE WORLD TODAY. WHERE IS HE? HOW DOES HE WORK?

He rescues and saves his people; he performs miraculous signs and wonders in the heavens and on earth. He has rescued Daniel from the power of the lions. DANIEL 6:27

God works to rescue and save his people.

It is the Lord who provides the sun to light the day and the moon and stars to light the night. It is he who stirs the sea into roaring waves. His name is the Lord Almighty. JEREMIAH 31:35

WHAT DOES GOD'S HAND BRING TO ME HERE IN THIS WORLD TODAY?

But Job replied, "—Should we accept only good things from the hand of God and never anything bad?" JOB 2:10

Sometimes God withdraws his hand and allows bad things to happen to good people. Why? Because his long-range eternal plans for your greater good may not fit your short-range view of comfort.

The LORD is close
to the brokenhearted;

he RESCUES
those who are

crushed in spirit.

Psalm 34:18

HAPPINESS

The godly can look forward to happiness, while the wicked can expect only wrath. Proverbs 11:23

HOW CAN I BE HAPPY IN THE MIDST OF THESE TROUBLED TIMES?

Since I know it is all for Christ's good, I am quite content with my weaknesses and with insults, hardships, persecutions, and calamities. For when I am weak, then I am strong. 2 CORINTHIANS 12:10

Dear friends, don't be surprised at the fiery trials you are going through, as if something strange were happening to you. Instead, be very glad—because ... you will have the wonderful joy of sharing his glory. 1 PETER 4:12-13

Difficult circumstances help you to better understand what Christ went through for you.

How beautiful on the mountains are the feet of those who bring good news of peace and salvation, the news that the God of Israel reigns! ISAIAH 52:7

Happiness is living and sharing the wonderful news about the Lord. And during days like these, that's what people need more than anything else!

Those who are wise will shine as bright as the sky, and those who turn many to righteousness will shine like stars forever. DANIEL 12:3

HATRED

You love what is right and hate what is wrong. Therefore God, your God, has anointed you, pouring out the oil of joy on you more than on anyone else. Psalm 45:7

IS IT EVER APPROPRIATE TO HATE ANYONE OR ANYTHING?

You who love the LORD, hate evil! PSALM 97:10

You have heard that the law of Moses says, "Love your neighbor" and hate your enemy. But I say, love your enemies! MATTHEW 5:43-44

Christians are to love all people and to hate all sin. When you truly love God, you will hate sin, because sin separates people from God and damages relationships with others. Hatred of people, however, is a sin. If you hate a person, you are most likely hating some kind of sin that that person committed against you. Hate the sin, but ask God to give you love for the sinner by enabling you to pray for that person.

HOW CAN I LET GO OF HATRED?

A gentle answer turns away wrath, but harsh words stir up anger. PROVERBS 15:1

This is what he requires: to do what is right, to love mercy, and to walk humbly with your God. MICAH 6:8

Mercy and humility are powerful weapons against hatred.

HEALING

But for you who fear my name, the Sun of Righteousness will rise with healing in his wings. And you will go free, leaping with joy like calves let out to pasture. Malachi 4:2

HOW DOES GOD HEAL?

"Make an ointment from figs and spread it over the boil." They did this, and Hezekiah recovered! 2 KINGS 20:7

Through physicians and medicine.

"Lord," he said, "if you want to, you can make me well again." Jesus reached out and touched the man. "I want to," he said. "Be healed!" LUKE 5:12-13

Through miracles.

Are any among you sick? They should call for the elders of the church and have them pray over them. JAMES 5:14

Through prayer.

He was wounded and crushed for our sins. He was beaten that we might have peace. He was whipped, and we were healed! ISAIAH 53:5

Through Christ. His death brought you life; his wounds brought you healing. By accepting your punishment, he set you free.

WHY DOESN'T GOD ALWAYS HEAL PEOPLE?

My power works best in your weakness. 2 CORINTHIANS 12:9

HEAVEN

No eye has seen, no ear has heard, and no mind has imagined what God has prepared for those who love him. 1 Corinthians 2:9

IS THERE REALLY A HEAVEN?

There are many rooms in my Father's home, and I am going to prepare a place for you. If this were not so, I would tell you plainly. JOHN 14:2

For we know that when this earthly tent we live in is taken down—when we die and leave these bodies—we will have a home in heaven. 2 CORINTHIANS 5:1

WHAT IS HEAVEN LIKE?

Look! I am creating new heavens and a new earth—so wonderful that no one will even think about the old ones anymore. ISAIAH 65:17

He will take these weak mortal bodies of ours and change them into glorious bodies like his own. PHILIPPIANS 3:21

I heard a loud shout from the throne, saying, "Look, the home of God is now among his people! He will live with them, and they will be his people. God himself will be with them. He will remove all of their sorrows, and there will be no more death or sorrow or crying or pain. For the old world and its evils are gone forever." REVELATION 21:3-4

But for you who fear my name, the

SUN OF

Righteousness

will rise with healing

in his WINGS.

And you will
go free,

LEAPING

with *joy*

like calves let out
to pasture.

Malachi 4:2

HELP

Be sure of this: I am with you always,
even to the end of the age. Matthew 28:20

I NEED HELP. WHAT KIND OF HELP CAN I EXPECT TO GET FROM GOD?

But whenever you were in distress and turned to the LORD ... and sought him out, you found him.
2 CHRONICLES 15:4

God is present to help you whenever you call to him. Prayer is the lifeline that connects you to the Lord God your helper.

This same God who takes care of me will supply all your needs from his glorious riches, which have been given to us in Christ Jesus. PHILIPPIANS 4:19

God has a full supply house and a ready supply system. It's free for the asking, but you must ask.

You will hear a voice say, "This is the way; turn around and walk here." ISAIAH 30:21

God guides you by his Holy Spirit.

LOTS OF PEOPLE NEED HELP. HOW CAN I HELP THEM?

When God's children are in need, be the one to help them out. And get into the habit of inviting guests home for dinner or, if they need lodging, for the night. ROMANS 12:13

HELPLESSNESS

Yes, the LORD is for me; he will help me. Psalm 118:7

WHAT CAN I DO WHEN I FEEL HELPLESS?

The Lord is my helper, so I will not be afraid. What can mere mortals do to me? HEBREWS 13:6

Meditate on God's limitless power and steadfast love for you, reminding yourself that the Lord is far greater than any problem confronting you.

But in my distress I cried out to the LORD; yes, I prayed to my God for help. He heard me from his sanctuary; my cry reached his ears. PSALM 18:6

Take time to reflect on past situations when you felt helpless but the Lord helped you. God's track record in your life can increase your confidence today.

HOW DOES GOD HELP ME WHEN I FEEL HELPLESS?

O Israel, trust the LORD! He is your helper; he is your shield. O priests of Aaron, trust the LORD! He is your helper; he is your shield. All you who fear the LORD, trust the LORD! He is your helper; he is your shield. PSALM 115:9-11

I am overwhelmed, and you alone know the way I should turn. Wherever I go, my enemies have set traps for me. PSALM 142:3

God gives direction. He who knows the way will lead you.

HOPE

"I know the plans I have for you," says the Lord.
*"They are plans for good and not for disaster, to
give you a future and a hope."* Jeremiah 29:11

WHERE DOES HOPE COME FROM?

And so, Lord, where do I put my hope? My only hope is in
you. PSALM 39:7

WHAT CAN I DO WHEN THINGS SEEM HOPELESS?

Hannah was in deep anguish, crying bitterly as she prayed
to the Lord. 1 SAMUEL 1:10

*You can pray. In the midst of Hannah's hopelessness, she prayed
to God, knowing that if any hope were to be found, it would be
found in him.*

He took no chances but put them into the inner dungeon
and clamped their feet in the stocks. Around midnight,
Paul and Silas were praying and singing hymns to God.
ACTS 16:24-25

*You can worship. Paul and Silas were on death row for preaching
about Jesus, yet in this hopeless situation they sang praises to God.
This reinforced an eternal perspective.*

Wait patiently for the Lord. Be brave and courageous.
PSALM 27:14

You can remember that God's timing is perfect.

HOSTILITY

My God is my rock, in whom I find protection. He is my shield, the strength of my salvation, and my stronghold, my high tower, my savior, the one who saves me from violence ... and rescues me from my enemies. You hold me safe beyond the reach of my enemies; you save me from violent opponents. 2 Samuel 22:3, 49

HOW CAN I HAVE PEACE INSTEAD OF HOSTILITY?

I have told you all this so that you may have peace in me. Here on earth you will have many trials and sorrows. But take heart, because I have overcome the world. JOHN 16:33

The secret of finding peace is to first seek it from the Prince of Peace. You can find the secret to peace in a personal relationship with Jesus Christ.

And so, dear friends, while you are waiting for these things to happen, make every effort to live a pure and blameless life. And be at peace with God. 2 PETER 3:14

Do your part to live in peace with everyone, as much as possible. ROMANS 12:18

God blesses those who work for peace, for they will be called the children of God. MATTHEW 5:9

Make peace a priority in your relationships—first with God, and then with others.

"I know the
PLANS
I have for you,"
says the LORD.
"They are plans for
GOOD
and not for disaster,
to give you a

FUTURE *&* a hope."

Jeremiah 29:11

HURTS

He will remove all of their sorrows, and there will be no more death or sorrow or crying or pain. For the old world and its evils are gone forever. Revelation 21:4

WHEN I'VE BEEN HURT, HOW CAN I FIND HEALING?

He has not ignored the suffering of the needy. He has not turned and walked away. He has listened to their cries for help. PSALM 22:24

Now let your unfailing love comfort me, just as you promised me, your servant. PSALM 119:76

God compassionately cares for you. Meditate on the attributes of his character and recognize that the one who made you is the best one to heal you.

HOW CAN I HELP PEOPLE WHO ARE HURTING?

Their insults have broken my heart, and I am in despair. If only one person would show some pity; if only one would turn and comfort me. PSALM 69:20

You can be aware of the effects of being brokenhearted on a person's spirit, mind, and body. Awareness leads to sympathy; sympathy leads to empathy; empathy leads to helping the wounded, and that leads to a time of healing.

IMPOSSIBLE

Now glory be to God! By his mighty power at work within us, he is able to accomplish infinitely more than we would ever dare to ask or hope. Ephesians 3:20

CAN GOD REALLY DO THE IMPOSSIBLE?

This is what the LORD Almighty says: All this may seem impossible to you now, a small and discouraged remnant of God's people. But do you think this is impossible for me, the LORD Almighty? ZECHARIAH 8:6

Jesus looked at them intently and said, "Humanly speaking, it is impossible. But with God everything is possible." MATTHEW 19:26

HOW DO I DEAL WITH IMPOSSIBLE SITUATIONS?

Trust in the LORD with all your heart; do not depend on your own understanding. PROVERBS 3:5

With God's help we will do mighty things, for he will trample down our foes. PSALM 60:12

"What do you mean, 'If I can'?" Jesus asked. "Anything is possible if a person believes." MARK 9:23

Place your faith and hope in God alone. Trust that God can do the impossible and have hope that he will. But even if he doesn't, believe that he is the only one who can.

He will judge the world with justice and
rule the nations with fairness. Psalm 9:8

WHAT WILL GOD DO ABOUT INJUSTICE?

You will bring justice to the orphans and the oppressed, so people can no longer terrify them. PSALM 10:18

The LORD replies, "I have seen violence done to the helpless, and I have heard the groans of the poor. Now I will rise up to rescue them, as they have longed for me to do."
PSALM 12:5

For the LORD loves justice, and he will never abandon the godly. He will keep them safe forever, but the children of the wicked will perish. PSALM 37:28

WHAT SHOULD I DO ABOUT INJUSTICE IN THE WORLD?

Give fair judgment to the poor and the orphan; uphold the rights of the oppressed and the destitute. PSALM 82:3

Speak up for those who cannot speak for themselves; ensure justice for those who are perishing. Yes, speak up for the poor and helpless, and see that they get justice.
PROVERBS 31:8-9

Learn to do good. Seek justice. Help the oppressed. Defend the orphan. Fight for the rights of widows. ISAIAH 1:17

The earnest prayer of a righteous person has great power and wonderful results. James 5:16

WHAT CAN I ASK FOR WHEN I'M INTERCEDING FOR SOMEONE?

Dear friend, I am praying that all is well with you and that your body is as healthy as I know your soul is. 3 JOHN 2

You can pray for the person's everyday, practical needs.

May the God of Israel grant the request you have asked of him. 1 SAMUEL 1:17

You can pray that God will satisfy the deepest longings of the person's heart.

Pray that I will be rescued from those in Judea who refuse to obey God. ROMANS 15:31

You can pray for the person to be delivered from a crisis.

"Pray to the Lord for me," Simon exclaimed, "that these terrible things won't happen to me!" ACTS 8:24

You can pray for the person's salvation.

Don't forget to pray for us, too, that God will give us many opportunities to preach about his secret plan—that Christ is also for you Gentiles. That is why I am here in chains. Pray that I will proclaim this message as clearly as I should. COLOSSIANS 4:3-4

JOY

The joy of the LORD is your strength! Nehemiah 8:10

WHAT IS THE SOURCE OF JOY?

But may all who search for you be filled with joy and gladness. May those who love your salvation repeatedly shout, "The LORD is great!" PSALM 40:16

Let the godly rejoice. Let them be glad in God's presence. Let them be filled with joy. PSALM 68:3

The Lord himself is the wellspring of true joy. The more you love him, know him, walk with him, and become like him, the greater your joy.

HOW CAN I BECOME MORE JOYFUL?

Happy are those who fear the LORD. Yes, happy are those who delight in doing what he commands. PSALM 112:1

Fear God and trust in him; delight in doing his commands.

I know the LORD is always with me ... No wonder my heart is filled with joy. PSALM 16:8-9

Joy comes from an awareness of God's presence, which brings true contentment.

But when the Holy Spirit controls our lives, he will produce this kind of fruit in us: love, joy ... GALATIANS 5:22

The presence of the Holy Spirit in your life produces joy.

JUSTICE

Never avenge yourselves. Leave that to God. For it is written, "I will take vengeance; I will repay those who deserve it," says the Lord. Romans 12:19

IS GOD ALWAYS FAIR AND JUST?

But God will use this persecution to show his justice ... and in his justice he will punish those who persecute you. 2 THESSALONIANS 1:5-6

When you are burdened with troubles, it is tempting to think that God is not fair or just. How can God allow a Christian to suffer when so many unbelievers are prospering? But rest assured that God's justice will eventually prevail.

THE WORLD SEEMS SO UNJUST. WILL GOD'S JUSTICE REALLY PREVAIL?

Let the trees of the forest rustle with praise before the LORD! For the LORD is coming! He is coming to judge the earth. He will judge the world with righteousness, and all the nations with his truth. PSALM 96:12-13

May your Kingdom come soon. May your will be done here on earth, just as it is in heaven. MATTHEW 6:10

Though complete justice will come only in the future, we can—and must—work for justice in our own spheres of influence. With God's help, justice will increase.

I know the

LORD

is always with me ...

No wonder my

heart

is filled with

JOY.

Psalm 16:8-9

LIMITATIONS

Glory be to God! By his mighty power at work within us, he is able to accomplish infinitely more than we would ever dare to ask or hope. Ephesians 3:20

DOES GOD HAVE ANY LIMITATIONS?

O LORD, you have examined my heart and know everything about me. You know when I sit down or stand up. You know my every thought when far away. You chart the path ahead of me and tell me where to stop and rest. Every moment you know where I am. You know what I am going to say even before I say it, LORD. You both precede and follow me. You place your hand of blessing on my head. Such knowledge is too wonderful for me, too great for me to know! PSALM 139:1-6

"My thoughts are completely different from yours," says the LORD. "And my ways are far beyond anything you could imagine." ISAIAH 55:8

God's knowledge has no limit. He is omniscient. He knows even our secret thoughts.

Jesus looked at them intently and said, "Humanly speaking, it is impossible. But with God everything is possible." MATTHEW 19:26

His great works are too marvelous to understand. He performs miracles without number. JOB 9:10

LOSS

The LORD is close to the brokenhearted; he rescues those who are crushed in spirit. Psalm 34:18

HOW DO I DEAL WITH LOSS IN MY LIFE?

Job stood up and tore his robe in grief ... He said, "–The LORD gave me everything I had, and the LORD has taken it away." JOB 1:20-21

Losses always bring pain. Recognizing and expressing your pain is not wrong or sinful, but is instead a healthy expression of how God created you.

I FEEL LIKE I'VE LOST EVERYTHING. WHERE CAN I TURN?

Have mercy on me, LORD, for I am in distress. My sight is blurred because of my tears. My body and soul are withering away. I am dying from grief; my years are shortened by sadness. Misery has drained my strength; I am wasting away from within. PSALM 31:9-10

I weep with grief; encourage me by your word. PSALM 119:28

He comforts us in all our troubles so that we can comfort others. When others are troubled, we will be able to give them the same comfort God has given us.
2 CORINTHIANS 1:4

Turn to God's people in times of loss, for they can give you God's counsel.

MOURNING

God blesses those who mourn, for they
will be comforted. Matthew 5:4

HOW LONG DOES MOURNING THE LOSS OF A LOVED ONE USUALLY LAST?

When Sarah was 127 years old, she died at Kiriath-arba (now called Hebron) in the land of Canaan. There Abraham mourned and wept for her. GENESIS 23:1-2

You can expect that the loss of a loved one will prompt deep and difficult emotions.

Weeping may go on all night, but joy comes with the morning. PSALM 30:5

God's Word assures us that mourning will not continue forever. Though you may always have a sense of loss, the pain will eventually subside.

He will remove all of their sorrows, and there will be no more death or sorrow or crying or pain. For the old world and its evils are gone forever. REVELATION 21:4

You can eagerly look forward to eternity, where death and mourning will be permanently eliminated.

OPPRESSION

The LORD is a shelter for the oppressed,
a refuge in times of trouble. Psalm 9:9

DOES GOD CARE ABOUT OPPRESSED PEOPLE?

He will help the oppressed, who have no one to defend them. PSALM 72:12

I will deal severely with all who have oppressed you. ZEPHANIAH 3:19

The Spirit of the Lord is upon me, for he has appointed me to preach Good News to the poor. He has sent me to proclaim that captives will be released, that the blind will see, that the downtrodden will be freed from their oppressors, and that the time of the Lord's favor has come. LUKE 4:18-19

I'M ONLY ONE PERSON. WHAT CAN I DO ABOUT OPPRESSION?

Give justice to the king, O God, and righteousness to the king's son ... Help him to defend the poor, to rescue the children of the needy, and to crush their oppressors.
PSALM 72:1, 4

Pray that your leaders will protect the weak and punish any who oppress them. Pray for the leaders of other countries to be fair and just, and to refuse to oppress any of their people.

The Lord is a
shelter
for the oppressed,
a REFUGE
in times of trouble.

Psalm 9:9

OVERCOMING

No, despite all these things, overwhelming victory is ours through Christ, who loved us. Romans 8:37

CAN I REALLY OVERCOME THE OBSTACLES AND ENEMIES I FACE?

Here on earth you will have many trials and sorrows. But take heart, because I have overcome the world. JOHN 16:33

Every child of God defeats this evil world by trusting Christ to give the victory. And the ones who win this battle against the world are the ones who believe that Jesus is the Son of God. 1 JOHN 5:4-5

HOW CAN I OVERCOME DIFFICULTIES IN MY LIFE?

Death had its hands around my throat; the terrors of the grave overtook me. I saw only trouble and sorrow. Then I called on the name of the LORD: "Please, LORD, save me!" How kind the LORD is! How good he is! So merciful, this God of ours! PSALM 116:3-5

Prayer is essential to winning the victory.

We are pressed on every side by troubles, but we are not crushed or broken. We are perplexed, but we don't give up and quit. We are hunted down, but God never abandons us. We get knocked down, but we get up again and keep going. 2 CORINTHIANS 4:8-9

OVERWHELMED

I am overwhelmed, and you alone know
the way I should turn. Psalm 142:3

HOW DOES GOD HELP ME WHEN I AM OVERWHELMED?

I am leaving you with a gift—peace of mind and heart. And the peace I give isn't like the peace the world gives. So don't be troubled or afraid. JOHN 14:27

As pressure and stress bear down on me, I find joy in your commands. PSALM 119:143

God's Word brings deep joy and contentment in the midst of overwhelming circumstances. God's Word will overcome whatever overwhelms you.

HOW DO I COPE WHEN LIFE'S PAIN BECOMES OVERWHELMING?

The LORD helps the fallen and lifts up those bent beneath their loads. PSALM 145:14

Why am I discouraged? Why so sad? I will put my hope in God! I will praise him again—my Savior and my God! PSALM 42:5-6

Those who plant in tears will harvest with shouts of joy. They weep as they go to plant their seed, but they sing as they return with the harvest. PSALM 126:5-6

PAIN

All praise to the God and Father of our Lord Jesus Christ. He is the source of every mercy and the God who comforts us. 2 Corinthians 1:3

HOW DOES GOD HELP ME DEAL WITH MY PAIN?

Give all your worries and cares to God, for he cares about what happens to you. 1 PETER 5:7

Now let your unfailing love comfort me, just as you promised me, your servant. PSALM 119:76

He heals the brokenhearted, binding up their wounds. PSALM 147:3

WHAT WILL HEAL MY PAIN?

I weep with grief; encourage me by your word ... Your promise revives me; it comforts me in all my troubles ... I meditate on your age-old laws; O LORD, they comfort me ... If your law hadn't sustained me with joy, I would have died in my misery. PSALM 119:28, 50, 52, 92

We have been greatly comforted, dear brothers and sisters, in all of our own crushing troubles and suffering, because you have remained strong in your faith. It gives us new life, knowing you remain strong in the Lord. 1 THESSALONIANS 3:7-8

PANIC

Don't be afraid, for I am with you. Do not be dismayed,
for I am your God. I will strengthen you. I will help you. I will
uphold you with my victorious right hand. Isaiah 41:10

WHAT CAN HELP ME WHEN I AM PANICKING?

Can all your worries add a single moment to your life? Of course not. And why worry about your clothes? Look at the lilies and how they grow. They don't work or make their clothing, yet Solomon in all his glory was not dressed as beautifully as they are. And if God cares so wonderfully for flowers that are here today and gone tomorrow, won't he more surely care for you? MATTHEW 6:27-30

God's promise to take care of you.

The Father who knows all hearts knows what the Spirit is saying, for the Spirit pleads for us believers in harmony with God's own will. ROMANS 8:27

I lay down and slept. I woke up in safety, for the LORD was watching over me. I am not afraid of ten thousand enemies who surround me on every side. PSALM 3:5-6

Literally, rest in the Lord. When you realize God is in control, you can sleep at night.

PEACE

*I am leaving you with a gift—peace
of mind and heart. John 14:27*

HOW CAN I GET INNER PEACE?

There will be glory and honor and peace from God for all who do good. ROMANS 2:10

You will keep in perfect peace all who trust in you, whose thoughts are fixed on you! ISAIAH 26:3

Those who are gentle and lowly will possess the land; they will live in prosperous security. PSALM 37:11

Those who love your law have great peace and do not stumble. PSALM 119:165

But when the Holy Spirit controls our lives, he will produce this kind of fruit in us: ... peace ... GALATIANS 5:22

IS THERE ANY HOPE FOR WORLD PEACE?

The LORD will settle international disputes. All the nations will beat their swords into plowshares and their spears into pruning hooks. All wars will stop, and military training will come to an end. MICAH 4:3

God blesses those who work for peace, for they will be called the children of God. MATTHEW 5:9

PERSECUTION

Don't be afraid of what you are about to suffer ...
Remain faithful even when facing death, and I will
give you the crown of life. Revelation 2:10

WHERE CAN I FIND HOPE WHEN I AM PERSECUTED?

Everyone who wants to live a godly life in Christ Jesus will suffer persecution. 2 TIMOTHY 3:12

The apostles left the high council rejoicing that God had counted them worthy to suffer dishonor for the name of Jesus. ACTS 5:41

God blesses you when you are mocked and persecuted and lied about because you are my followers. MATTHEW 5:11

Jesus promises special blessings to those who are persecuted for his sake.

AS A CHRISTIAN, HOW SHOULD I RESPOND WHEN I AM PERSECUTED FOR MY FAITH?

If people persecute you because you are a Christian, don't curse them; pray that God will bless them. ROMANS 12:14

Pray that God will bless those who persecute you, for it may be through your godly response to their persecution that God touches a hard heart and turns it to him.

You will keep in

perfect
PEACE

all who

TRUST in you,

whose thoughts are
fixed on you!

Isaiah 26:3

*The earnest prayer of a righteous person has
great power and wonderful results. James 5:16*

WHAT IS PRAYER?

If my people who are called by my name will humble themselves and pray and seek my face and turn from their wicked ways, I will hear from heaven. 2 CHRONICLES 7:14

If we confess our sins to him, he is faithful and just to forgive us and to cleanse us from every wrong. 1 JOHN 1:9

The next morning Jesus awoke long before daybreak and went out alone into the wilderness to pray. MARK 1:35

Prayer is an expression of an intimate relationship with your Father, who makes his love and resources available to you.

DOES GOD ALWAYS ANSWER PRAYER?

Three different times I begged the Lord to take it away. Each time he said, "... My power works best in your weakness." 2 CORINTHIANS 12:8-9

We can be confident that he will listen to us whenever we ask him for anything in line with his will. 1 JOHN 5:14

Praying in Jesus' name means praying according to Jesus' character and purposes. When you pray like this, you are asking for what God already wants to give you.

PREJUDICE

There is no longer Jew or Gentile, slave or free, male or female. For you are all Christians—you are one in Christ Jesus. Galatians 3:28

WHAT KIND OF PREJUDICE DOES GOD CONDEMN?

Don't judge by his appearance or height … The Lord doesn't make decisions the way you do! People judge by outward appearance, but the Lord looks at a person's thoughts and intentions. 1 SAMUEL 16:7

God condemns prejudice based on outward appearance. It is wrong to judge a person by the outward appearance; the real person inside may be quite different from how they appear.

But if you pay special attention to the rich, you are committing a sin. JAMES 2:9

God condemns prejudice based on financial well-being or socioeconomic class. Money is not a measure of character.

Don't let anyone think less of you because you are young. 1 TIMOTHY 4:12

Never speak harshly to an older man, but appeal to him respectfully as though he were your own father. Talk to the younger men as you would to your own brothers. 1 TIMOTHY 5:1

The Bible forbids discrimination based on age. Maturity is not always a by-product of age.

PRESENCE OF GOD

I will be your God throughout your lifetime—until your hair is white with age. I made you, and I will care for you. I will carry you along and save you. Isaiah 46:4

HOW CAN I EXPERIENCE GOD'S PRESENCE FOR TODAY ON EARTH AND FOR ETERNITY IN HEAVEN?

Look! Here I stand at the door and knock. If you hear me calling and open the door, I will come in, and we will share a meal as friends. REVELATION 3:20

Then he said, "I assure you, unless you turn from your sins and become as little children, you will never get into the Kingdom of Heaven." MATTHEW 18:3

WHAT SHOULD I DO WHEN IT FEELS LIKE GOD IS FAR AWAY?

I know the LORD is always with me. I will not be shaken, for he is right beside me. PSALM 16:8

God's presence is with you regardless of life's circumstances.

I can never escape from your spirit! I can never get away from your presence! PSALM 139:7

God will go to any height or depth to be with you—he is always by your side. Don't trust your feelings; trust God's promises.

PROBLEMS

Don't worry about anything; instead, pray about everything. Tell God what you need, and thank him for all he has done. Philippians 4:6

HOW DOES GOD VIEW MY PROBLEMS?

Give all your worries and cares to God, for he cares about what happens to you. 1 PETER 5:7

The LORD helps the fallen and lifts up those bent beneath their loads. PSALM 145:14

HOW CAN I BEST COPE WITH LIFE'S PROBLEMS?

But when I am afraid, I put my trust in you. O God, I praise your word. I trust in God, so why should I be afraid? What can mere mortals do to me? PSALM 56:3-4

But Jesus ignored their comments and said to Jairus, "Don't be afraid. Just trust me." MARK 5:36

Seeking God's solutions for your problems can enhance your faith, praise, and joy.

We can rejoice, too, when we run into problems and trials, for we know that they are good for us—they help us learn to endure. And endurance develops strength of character in us, and character strengthens our confident expectation of salvation. ROMANS 5:3-4

But when I am afraid,
I put my *trust* in you.
O God, I praise your word.
I TRUST IN GOD,
so why should I be afraid?
What can mere mortals
do to me?

Psalm 56:3-4

PROMISES

Without wavering, let us hold tightly to the hope we say we have, for God can be trusted to keep his promise. Hebrews 10:23

HOW SHOULD GOD'S PROMISES IMPACT MY LIFE?

So God has given us both his promise and his oath. These two things are unchangeable because it is impossible for God to lie. Therefore, we who have fled to him for refuge can take new courage, for we can hold on to his promise with confidence. HEBREWS 6:18

God's promises should prompt you to obedience. The promise of Christ's imminent return is also a great motivation for Christian conduct!

WITH SO LITTLE TO DEPEND ON IN LIFE, WHAT CAN I COUNT ON FROM GOD?

The Spirit is God's guarantee that he will give us everything he promised. EPHESIANS 1:14

You can count on getting everything God has promised because of the Holy Spirit's presence in your life. The Holy Spirit is God's guarantee that his promises are trustworthy.

We know that God causes everything to work together for the good of those who love God and are called according to his purpose for them. ROMANS 8:28

PROTECTION

For he orders his angels to protect you wherever you go.

Psalm 91:11

DOES GOD PROMISE TO PROTECT ME?

Guard me as the apple of your eye … When I awake, I will be fully satisfied, for I will see you face to face. PSALM 17:8, 15

The psalmist prayed to God for protection from his enemies, yet trusted that ultimate safety is God's salvation, which leads to the hope of heaven.

His peace will guard your hearts and minds as you live in Christ Jesus. PHILIPPIANS 4:7

Through consistent and devoted prayer, you can know the protection of God's supernatural peace.

But if you refuse to obey the LORD … the war and famine you fear will follow close behind you. JEREMIAH 42:13, 16

Jeremiah teaches the relationship between obedience and the protection of God. Obedience to God will protect you from the consequences of disobedience. For example, obeying God's command not to cheat will protect you from the embarrassment, loss of friendships, fines, and potential jail time that can come from cheating.

This same God who takes care of me will supply
all your needs from his glorious riches, which have
been given to us in Christ Jesus. Philippians 4:19

**WHAT DOES IT MEAN TO TRUST GOD'S PROVISION?
CAN I REALLY TRUST HIM TO TAKE CARE OF ME?**

Come and listen to what the LORD your God says.
Today you will know that the living God is among you.
JOSHUA 3:9-10

You can trust him to care for you if you are being obedient to him.

As we know Jesus better, his divine power gives us everything
we need for living a godly life. 2 PETER 1:3

*You can trust him to care for your spiritual needs. God has provided
resources from his own character to those who seek him.*

Jesus replied, "I am the bread of life. No one who comes to
me will ever be hungry again." JOHN 6:35

*You can trust him to fill your deepest hunger. God knows that what
you really need is to have your heart filled with the love and power
of Christ himself.*

QUITTING

And everyone will hate you because of your allegiance to me.
But those who endure to the end will be saved. Matthew 10:22

HOW CAN I KEEP GOING WHEN I FEEL LIKE QUITTING?

What does this bunch of poor, feeble Jews think they are doing? ... That stone wall would collapse if even a fox walked along the top of it! NEHEMIAH 4:2-3

You reach your goal when you keep yourself focused on it.

We are pressed on every side by troubles, but we are not crushed and broken. We are perplexed, but we don't give up and quit. 2 CORINTHIANS 4:8

Even in the midst of suffering, you can find strength to endure for Christ.

I have fought a good fight, I have finished the race, and I have remained faithful. 2 TIMOTHY 4:7

Don't get tired of doing what is good. Don't get discouraged and give up, for we will reap a harvest of blessing at the appropriate time. GALATIANS 6:9

You can avoid discouragement and the desire to quit by keeping your eyes on the goal and reward of heaven.

Don't get tired of doing what is *good.* Don't get discouraged and give up,

for we will reap a

HARVEST

of BLESSING

at the appropriate time.

Galatians 6:9

Create in me a clean heart, O God.
Renew a right spirit within me. Psalm 51:10

MY LIFE IS SUCH A MESS. I'M CONFUSED. HOW CAN I EXPERIENCE RENEWAL IN MY LIFE?

And I will give you a new heart with new and right desires, and I will put a new spirit in you. I will take out your stony heart of sin and give you a new, obedient heart. And I will put my Spirit in you so you will obey my laws and do whatever I command. EZEKIEL 36:26-27

Throw off your old evil nature and your former way of life, which is rotten through and through … Instead, there must be a spiritual renewal of your thoughts and attitudes. You must display a new nature because you are a new person, created in God's likeness—righteous, holy, and true. EPHESIANS 4:22-24

IN WHAT WAYS DOES GOD RENEW ME?

He renews my strength. He guides me along right paths, bringing honor to his name. PSALM 23:3

That is why we never give up. Though our bodies are dying, our spirits are being renewed every day. 2 CORINTHIANS 4:16

God renews your spirit.

He led me to a place of safety; he rescued
me because he delights in me. Psalm 18:19

FROM WHAT DOES GOD RESCUE ME?

He died for our sins, just as God our Father planned, in order to rescue us from this evil world in which we live. GALATIANS 1:4

All praise to him who loves us and has freed us from our sins by shedding his blood for us. REVELATION 1:5

I prayed to the LORD, and he answered me, freeing me from all my fears. PSALM 34:4

HOW DOES GOD RESCUE ME?

"Yes," says the LORD, "I will do mighty miracles for you, like those I did when I rescued you from slavery in Egypt." MICAH 7:15

He will rescue us because you are helping by praying for us. As a result, many will give thanks to God because so many people's prayers for our safety have been answered. 2 CORINTHIANS 1:11

God often rescues you with the help of people—believers and unbelievers—as his agents of rescue on your behalf.

The angel of the LORD guards all who fear
him, and he rescues them. Psalm 34:7

WILL GOD KEEP ME SAFE FROM PHYSICAL HARM?

For he orders his angels to protect you wherever you go.
PSALM 91:11

We can rejoice, too, when we run into problems and trials.
ROMANS 5:3

Choose to love the LORD your God and to obey him ...
Then you will live long in the land. DEUTERONOMY 30:20

Through his Word, God offers wisdom that helps you avoid needless peril.

IF GOD DOESN'T GUARANTEE PHYSICAL SAFETY, WHAT'S THE POINT OF FAITH?

They are not part of this world any more than I am.
JOHN 17:16

Faith has more to do with the eternal safety of your soul than the physical safety of your body.

I know the one in whom I trust, and I am sure that he is able to guard what I have entrusted to him until the day of his return. 2 TIMOTHY 1:12

If you confess with your mouth that Jesus is Lord
and believe in your heart that God raised him from
the dead, you will be saved. Romans 10:9

WHAT DOES IT MEAN TO BE SAVED?

What joy for those whose sin is no longer counted against them by the Lord. ROMANS 4:8

He has removed our rebellious acts as far away from us as the east is from the west. PSALM 103:12

Remove the stain of my guilt. Create in me a clean heart, O God. PSALM 51:9-10

Being saved means the stain of your guilt has been washed away. It not only appears to be gone, it is gone!

I assure you, those who listen to my message and believe in God who sent me have eternal life. JOHN 5:24

HOW CAN I BE SAVED?

For God so loved the world that he gave his only Son, so that everyone who believes in him will not perish but have eternal life. JOHN 3:16

Believe on the Lord Jesus and you will be saved. ACTS 16:31

If you confess
with your mouth that

Jesus **IS LORD**

and believe in your

HEART

that God raised him from
the dead, you will be
saved.

Romans 10:9

All who are victorious will be clothed in white. I will never erase their names from the Book of Life, but I will announce before my Father and his angels that they are mine. Revelation 3:5

HOW DOES GOD PROVIDE SECURITY?

Those who fear the LORD are secure; he will be a place of refuge for their children. PROVERBS 14:26

I follow close behind you; your strong right hand holds me securely. PSALM 63:8

No matter how much the storms of life batter you, you are eternally secure with God. Nothing can ever separate you from his eternal presence.

HOW CAN I FEEL SECURE ABOUT THE FUTURE?

Don't worry about anything; instead, pray about everything ... If you do this, you will experience God's peace, which is far more wonderful than the human mind can understand. PHILIPPIANS 4:6-7

Nothing in all creation will ever be able to separate us from the love of God. ROMANS 8:39

The most powerful security in the world is knowing that nothing can separate you from the love of God.

SORROW

He will swallow up death forever! The Sovereign
Lord will wipe away all tears. Isaiah 25:8

I HAVE TROUBLE RECONCILING THE SORROW AND GRIEF OF LIFE WITH THE LOVE OF GOD. IS GOD CONCERNED ABOUT MY PAIN?

He was despised and rejected—a man of sorrows.
ISAIAH 53:3

Then Jesus wept. The people who were standing nearby said, "See how much he loved him." JOHN 11:35-36

The tears of Jesus demonstrate that great grief comes from great love.

Give all your worries and cares to God, for he cares about what happens to you. 1 PETER 5:7

HOW CAN I FIND HOPE IN MY TIMES OF SORROW?

He will remove all of their sorrows, and there will be no more death or sorrow or crying or pain. REVELATION 21:4

I want you to know what will happen to the Christians who have died so you will not be full of sorrow like people who have no hope. 1 THESSALONIANS 4:13

He comforts us in all our troubles so that we can comfort others. 2 CORINTHIANS 1:4

The LORD is my strength, my shield from every danger. I trust in him with all my heart. He helps me, and my heart is filled with joy. I burst out in songs of thanksgiving. Psalm 28:7

HOW CAN I EXPERIENCE THE STRENGTH OF GOD IN MY LIFE?

I pray that you will begin to understand the incredible greatness of his power for us who believe him.
EPHESIANS 1:19-23

Don't be afraid, for I am with you. Do not be dismayed, for I am your God. I will strengthen you. I will help you. I will uphold you with my victorious right hand. ISAIAH 41:10

But when the Holy Spirit has come upon you, you will receive power and will tell people about me everywhere—in Jerusalem, throughout Judea, in Samaria, and to the ends of the earth. ACTS 1:8

HOW DO I TAP INTO GOD'S STRENGTH TO FIGHT THE BATTLES OF LIFE?

Fight the good fight for what we believe. Hold tightly to the eternal life that God has given you, which you have confessed so well before many witnesses. 1 TIMOTHY 6:12

I have fought a good fight, I have finished the race, and I have remained faithful. 2 TIMOTHY 4:7

I have told you all this so that you may have peace in me.
Here on earth you will have many trials and sorrows. But
take heart, because I have overcome the world. John 16:33

HOW CAN I DEAL WITH STRESS?

Give your burdens to the LORD, and he will take care of you.
He will not permit the godly to slip and fall. PSALM 55:22

Don't drink only water. You ought to drink a little wine for
the sake of your stomach because you are sick so often.
1 TIMOTHY 5:23

Take care of your body. Adequate rest, regular exercise, and proper
nutrition are useful tools for dealing with stress.

HOW DO I RESPOND TO STRESS SO THAT SOMETHING GOOD CAN COME FROM IT?

Dear brothers and sisters, whenever trouble comes your
way, let it be an opportunity for joy. For when your faith
is tested, your endurance has a chance to grow. So let it
grow, for when your endurance is fully developed, you will
be strong in character and ready for anything. JAMES 1:2-4

Character is built from the positive building blocks of life. What
you do with stress not only reveals your character but also helps
develop your character.

SUFFERING

Come back to the place of safety ... for there is yet hope! I promise this very day that I will repay you two mercies for each of your woes. Zechariah 9:12

WHY DO I EXPERIENCE SUFFERING? WHY DOES GOD LET ANYONE SUFFER?

My child, don't ignore it when the LORD disciplines you ... For the LORD corrects those he loves, just as a father corrects a child in whom he delights. PROVERBS 3:11-12

When your faith is tested, your endurance has a chance to grow. JAMES 1:3

CAN ANY GOOD COME FROM MY SUFFERING?

We can rejoice, too, when we run into problems and trials, for we know that they are good for us—they help us learn to endure. And endurance develops strength of character. ROMANS 5:3-4

All praise to the God and Father of our Lord Jesus Christ. He is the source of every mercy and the God who comforts us. He comforts us ... so that we can comfort others. 2 CORINTHIANS 1:3-4

Wounded healers are more welcome than healers who have never been wounded. Woundedness may appear to weaken you, but it actually better enables you to minister to the suffering.

SYMPATHY

Finally, all of you should be of one mind, full of sympathy toward each other, loving one another with tender hearts and humble minds. 1 Peter 3:8

DOES THE LORD REALLY SYMPATHIZE WITH ME IN MY TIME OF NEED?

The LORD is like a father to his children, tender and compassionate to those who fear him. For he understands how weak we are; he knows we are only dust. PSALM 103:13-14

This High Priest of ours understands our weaknesses, for he faced all of the same temptations we do, yet he did not sin. HEBREWS 4:15

The story of Jesus is a story of tender compassion toward those in need.

HOW CAN I SHOW SYMPATHY TO OTHERS?

"Now which of these three would you say was a neighbor to the man who was attacked by bandits?" Jesus asked. The man replied, "The one who showed him mercy." Then Jesus said, "Yes, now go and do the same." LUKE 10:36-37

When others are troubled, we will be able to give them the same comfort God has given us. 2 CORINTHIANS 1:4

The LORD is like a father
to his children,
TENDER and
compassionate
to those who fear him.

FOR HE UNDERSTANDS

how weak we are;
he knows we are only dust.

Psalm 103:13-14

TERRORISM

Don't be afraid, for I am with you. Do not be dismayed, for I am your God. I will strengthen you. I will help you. I will uphold you with my victorious right hand. Isaiah 41:10

HOW CAN I AVOID LIVING IN CONSTANT FEAR?

The LORD is my light and my salvation—so why should I be afraid? The LORD protects me from danger—so why should I tremble? PSALM 27:1

Don't be afraid of those who want to kill you. They can only kill your body; they cannot touch your soul. MATTHEW 10:28

Remembering that your eternity is secure in Christ and untouchable by terrorists can build your confidence.

So don't worry about tomorrow, for tomorrow will bring its own worries. Today's trouble is enough for today. MATTHEW 6:34

HOW SHOULD I PRAY IN THIS TIME OF TERRORISM?

You have heard that the law of Moses says, "Love your neighbor" and hate your enemy. But I say, love your enemies! Pray for those who persecute you. MATTHEW 5:43-44

You can pray that terrorists will find God's love and that their lives will be transformed. This is not contradictory to the prayer that God will judge terrorists since both mercy and justice are part of God's character.

THANKFULNESS

Praise the LORD! How good it is to sing praises to our God! How delightful and how right! Psalm 147:1

WHAT CAN I BE THANKFUL FOR?

Jesus took the five loaves and two fish, looked up toward heaven, and asked God's blessing on the food. MARK 6:41

You can thank God for his provision of life's basic needs, such as food, clothing, shelter, and life itself.

But I trust in your unfailing love. I will rejoice because you have rescued me. I will sing to the LORD because he has been so good to me. PSALM 13:5-6

Whatever is good and perfect comes to us from God above, who created all heaven's lights. Unlike them, he never changes or casts shifting shadows. JAMES 1:17

ARE THERE THINGS I CAN BE THANKFUL FOR EVEN WHEN CIRCUMSTANCES ARE NOT GOING WELL?

Give thanks to the LORD, for he is good! His faithful love endures forever. 1 CHRONICLES 16:34

How we thank God, who gives us victory over sin and death through Jesus Christ our Lord! 1 CORINTHIANS 15:57

Thank God for his Son—a gift too wonderful for words! 2 CORINTHIANS 9:15

TIMING OF GOD

These things I plan won't happen right away.
Slowly, steadily, surely, the time approaches
when the vision will be fulfilled. If it seems slow,
wait patiently, for it will surely take place.
It will not be delayed. Habakkuk 2:3

HOW CAN I BE PATIENT AS I WAIT FOR GOD'S TIMING?

You are my strength; I wait for you to rescue me, for you, O God, are my place of safety. PSALM 59:9

Remind yourself continually of God's faithfulness. He is actively working in your life to help you become all he made you to be.

Be glad for all God is planning for you. Be patient in trouble, and always be prayerful. ROMANS 12:12

Be steadfast in prayer.

TRAGEDY

"For I know the plans I have for you," says the LORD.
*"They are plans for good and not for disaster, to
give you a future and a hope."* Jeremiah 29:11

HOW DOES GOD HELP IN TIMES OF TRAGEDY?

LORD, you know the hopes of the helpless. Surely you will listen to their cries and comfort them. PSALM 10:17

Morning, noon, and night I plead aloud in my distress, and the LORD hears my voice. PSALM 55:17

God listens to your prayers.

In my distress I prayed to the LORD, and the LORD answered me and rescued me. PSALM 118:5

Let your unfailing love surround us, LORD, for our hope is in you alone. PSALM 33:22

HOW SHOULD I HANDLE TRAGEDY?

I cry out to God without holding back. Oh, that God would listen to me! PSALM 77:1

I took my troubles to the LORD; I cried out to him, and he answered my prayer. PSALM 120:1

Trust me in your times of trouble, and I will rescue you, and you will give me glory. PSALM 50:15

The LORD is good. When trouble comes, he is a strong refuge.
And he knows everyone who trusts in him. Nahum 1:7

HOW SHOULD I RESPOND WHEN TROUBLE COMES?

As pressure and stress bear down on me, I find joy in your commands. PSALM 119:143

Don't worry about tomorrow, for tomorrow will bring its own worries. Today's trouble is enough for today. MATTHEW 6:34

Share each other's troubles and problems, and in this way obey the law of Christ. GALATIANS 6:2

HOW DOES GOD HELP ME IN MY TIMES OF TROUBLE?

My problems go from bad to worse. Oh, save me from them all! PSALM 25:17

God is bigger than any trouble you may face. Nothing surprises him, scares him, or intimidates him.

Do not stay so far from me, for trouble is near, and no one else can help me. PSALM 22:11

God knows all about your trouble and is ready to help you.

The LORD hears his people when they call to him for help. He rescues them from all their troubles. PSALM 34:17

Give all your worries and cares to God, for he cares about what happens to you. 1 PETER 5:7

You will keep in perfect peace all who trust in you,
whose thoughts are fixed on you! Isaiah 26:3

WHY SHOULD I PUT MY TRUST IN GOD? HOW DO I KNOW HE IS TRUSTWORTHY?

God is not a man, that he should lie. NUMBERS 23:19

This truth gives them the confidence of eternal life, which God promised before the world began—and he cannot lie. TITUS 1:2

The unfailing love of the LORD never ends! LAMENTATIONS 3:22

WHY SHOULD I TRUST GOD?

We know how much God loves us, and we have put our trust in him. God is love, and all who live in love live in God, and God lives in them. 1 JOHN 4:16

Those who know your name trust in you, for you, O LORD, have never abandoned anyone who searches for you. PSALM 9:10

The LORD's delight is in those who honor him, those who put their hope in his unfailing love. PSALM 147:11

Jesus Christ is the same yesterday, today, and forever. HEBREWS 13:8

Give all your worries and cares to

GOD,

for he cares about what happens to you.

1 Peter 5:7

WAR

God blesses those who work for peace, for they will be called the children of God. Matthew 5:9

WHAT DOES GOD THINK OF WAR?

So God created people in his own image; God patterned them after himself; male and female he created them. GENESIS 1:27

The LORD's loved ones are precious to him; it grieves him when they die. PSALM 116:15

God created every person and God loves every person. Therefore, anything that takes human life grieves God. So even if we conclude there are times when war is permissible or necessary, remember that war should always be our last resort.

WILL GOD EVER DO ANYTHING ABOUT WAR?

The LORD will settle international disputes. All the nations will beat their swords into plowshares and their spears into pruning hooks. All wars will stop, and military training will come to an end. MICAH 4:3

Come, see the glorious works of the LORD: See how he brings destruction upon the world and causes wars to end throughout the earth. He breaks the bow and snaps the spear in two; he burns the shields with fire. PSALM 46:8-9

WISDOM

*Come here and listen to me! I'll pour out the spirit of
wisdom upon you and make you wise. Proverbs 1:23*

HOW WILL HAVING WISDOM HELP ME?

Since a dull ax requires great strength, sharpen the blade.
That's the value of wisdom; it helps you succeed.
ECCLESIASTES 10:10

Wisdom will help you to succeed in what you do.

Be careful how you live, not as fools but as those who are
wise. EPHESIANS 5:15

Wisdom will multiply your days and add years to your life. If
you become wise, you will be the one to benefit. If you
scorn wisdom, you will be the one to suffer. PROVERBS 9:11-12

Wisdom will give you a more fulfilling life.

HOW DO I OBTAIN WISDOM?

If you need wisdom … ask him, and he will gladly tell you.
He will not resent your asking. JAMES 1:5

The fear of the Lord is true wisdom; to forsake evil is real
understanding. JOB 28:28

Fear of the LORD is the beginning of wisdom. Knowledge of
the Holy One results in understanding. PROVERBS 9:10

WORRY

*Give all your worries and cares to God, for he cares
about what happens to you.* 1 Peter 5:7

WHEN DOES WORRY BECOME SIN?

The thorny ground represents those who hear and accept
the Good News, but all too quickly the message is crowded
out by the cares of this life. MATTHEW 13:22

Let heaven fill your thoughts. Do not think only about
things down here on earth. COLOSSIANS 3:2

*Worry over the concerns of life becomes sin when it prevents the
Word of God from taking root in your life.*

WHY DO I WORRY SO MUCH? HOW CAN I WORRY LESS?

Don't worry about anything; instead, pray about everything.
PHILIPPIANS 4:6

You can combat worry by placing your cares in Jesus' hands.

He alone is my rock and my salvation, my fortress where I
will not be shaken. PSALM 62:6

You can find relief from fear in the promise of salvation.

Can all your worries add a single moment to your life?
MATTHEW 6:27

*Your worries lose their grip on you as you focus on kingdom
priorities.*